SURVIVING NURSING SCHOOL & BEYOND

A Prayer and Devotional for Novice & Advanced Practice Student Nurses

By

Tomekia Y. Luckett, PhD, RN

Also including:

Learning strategies

Classroom strategies

Test- taking strategies

Clinical Strategies

Strategies for Advanced practice students

Foreword written by: Ashley (A.G Nursing for All) Autman -Griffin MSN, BSN, RN

Copyright Notice

Tomekia Luckett, PhD, RN

Surviving Nursing School & Beyond: A Prayer & Devotional For Student And Graduate Nurses

© 2020, Tomekia Y. Luckett, PhD, RN

Dr. Tomekia Yvette Enterprises LLC

www.drtomekia.com

ALL RIGHTS RESERVED. This book contains material protected under International and Federal Copyright Laws and Treaties. Any unauthorized reprint or use of this material is prohibited. No part of this book may be reproduced or transmitted in any form or by any means, electronic or mechanical, including photocopying, recording, or by any information storage and retrieval system without express written permission from the author / publisher.

This book contains material protected under International and Federal Copyright Laws and Treaties. Any unauthorized reprint or use of this material is prohibited. No part of this book may be reproduced or transmitted in any form or by any means, electronic or mechanical, including photocopying, recording, or by any information storage and retrieval system without express written permission from the author/publisher.

I have tried to recreate events, locales and conversations from my memories of them. In order to maintain their anonymity in some instances, I have changed the names of individuals and places and I may have changed some identifying characteristics and details such as physical properties, occupations and places of residence.

Although the author and publisher have made every effort to ensure that the information in this book was correct at press time, the author and publisher do not assume and hereby disclaim any liability to any party for any loss, damage, or disruption caused by errors or omissions, whether such errors or omissions result from negligence, accident, or any other cause.

Scriptures marked KJV are taken from the KING JAMES VERSION (KJV): KING JAMES

VERSION, public domain.

Scripture quotations, marked NIV are taken from The Holy Bible, New International Version ®, NIV ®, Copyright 1973, 1978, 1984, 2001 by Biblica, Inc.™ Used by permission. All rights reserved.

DEDICATION

To Jehovah, the true and living God, the most high God who was, who is and who is to come. You are the source of my strength and my joy. Truly, without Your precious Spirit this would not be possible. To You alone, Lord I am forever grateful!

To the wonderful students who I have taught through the years, you inspired me to share my love and passion for nursing education with the next generation of nurses.

To my sons, Tamerrious, Tamerrion, and Tamerrick my endeavor is to continue to make you three proud. You three are my greatest inspiration, and motivation to continually pursue excellence.

To the toughest soldier I have ever known, you fought a good fight, kept the faith, and finished your course. Thank you for always being my friend, you are missed!

To the future generations of nurses, may you always remember that, **with *God, all things are possible***!

TABLE OF CONTENTS

Foreword 1

Introduction 3

Day One ~ The Law 5

Day Two ~ The Promise 7

Day 3 ~ God's Secret Weapon 9

Day 4 ~ He Is Greater 11

Day 5 ~ The Word 13

Day 6 ~ He Walks On Water 15

Day 7 ~ Recovering All 17

Day 8 ~ Don't Be Afraid 19

Day 9 ~ Send Up Praise 21

Day 10 ~ Victory On The Cross 23

Day 11 ~ God Is With You 25

Day 12 ~ God Who Answers By Fire 27

Day 13 ~ A Heavenly Host Is With You 29

Day 14 ~ Hope In Jesus 31

Day 15 ~ Words Have Power 33

Nursing Student Tips 36

Learning Strategies 38

Classroom Strategies 41

Test Taking Strategies 43

Clinical Strategies 46

FOREWORD

Being asked to complete life-changing, high-priority tasks can be exciting, overwhelming, frightening, and honestly, downright daunting. Nursing school has a way of exposing every doubt, insecurity and shortcoming we have. Being entrusted to write the foreword for a loved and respected colleague and friend's work feels quite similar.

Dr. Tomekia is more than simply loved and respected as my friend. Aside from being a phenomenal nurse, teacher, mother, woman and dynamic speaker, she has served as my mentor, my role model, and my example of everything that is right in the nursing profession. They say that you make friends for life as you journey through nursing school; that is, without a doubt, the understatement of the year.

I met Dr. Tomekia at William Carey University, where we were both pursuing our Masters in Nursing Education. Our first of many classes together was Advanced Pathophysiology. If you ask me how I remember this, the answer is simple. There are people and moments in your life that are permanently etched in your memory. You can easily relive the moment and see it play out in your mind.

One of our big assignments for this course was to "teach" a topic from Pathophysiology to our classmates and Professor. I was immediately concerned, because "Patho" was a weak spot for me. It was the class I had to repeat in nursing school. If I did not really understand it then, how in the world was I going to teach it?

I worked on the assignment for weeks and felt prepared, yet apprehensive about presenting it. I soldiered through it. I remember Dr. Tomekia was sitting near the front and she was very actively engaged in my lecture, so I made sure to make a lot of eye contact with her. At the end of my presentation, the Professor asked a few questions and as I made my way to my seat, Dr. Tomekia stopped me. What she said to me that day changed the way I thought about everything, and her kindness has propelled me throughout my career as a nursing educator.

Friends, I questioned my ability; not just my ability to complete the assignment, but my full ability and worthiness to be an educator. Who was I to think I could do this? I struggled in nursing school. How was someone who barely made it out going to teach future nurses? Dr. Tomekia looked at me and asked, "Have you taught before? You've done this before." My response was, "No. This was my first time ever doing a lecture like this." Her next words have fueled me, even to this point. "Well, you would never know! You did a great job and you're a natural!" It must have been the way she said it or the look in her eyes as she said it, because I believed her.

Dr. Tomekia was destined to lead future nurses and influence the nursing culture. The calling that God has placed on her life is evident; and the impact that she has had, and will continue to have, on the future of nursing is profound. Her ability to encourage a young, future nursing educator, who questioned her ability and worthiness to teach and lead future nurses, has led to a life's work of change, accomplishment, and advancement of the nursing profession. I honestly believe that God used Dr. Tomekia to change the entire course of a life that day. It is also my belief that He will use her again through this work. Future nurses, you have a great calling upon your life. Let God's promises in this devotional speak to your heart. Let it carry you through every disappointment, short-coming, and heart-break that nursing school may bring. Let it also help you to lift up a praise for every celebration, victory, and fulfilling moment of your journey to becoming the life-saving and life-changing nurse you are called to be.

To God be the glory,

Ashley Autman-Griffin, MSN, RN

Creator of Nursing For All

INTRODUCTION

The decision to become a nurse or advance in your nursing career is perhaps one of the most important and life changing decisions you will ever make. As a nurse educator, I have been afforded the distinct privilege of educating nurses across all levels, including practical nursing through to the doctoral level. Though the educational paths are varied, there are a few common features. Common features include the necessity of being self-motivated. Self-motivation is essential for the days when you want to quit. My educational journey initially began nearly twenty years ago in pursuit of my associate degree and it was extremely challenging as at the time, I was a single mother of medically fragile triplets. I learned early on to become organized and my mantra was and remains "Failure is not an option." I learned during those times to rely on the power of prayer and to believe God for the impossible. The possibilities in life and a career are unlimited when you believe. As the journey continued, I knew God destined me for greater. I began teaching nursing at the practical nursing level in 2009 and knew immediately I had found my purpose. I knew teaching was more than a job - it was my passion. In that moment, I knew returning to school was my only option. As an adult learner balancing husband, children and career, my challenges differed from my classmates. However, my determination and will to pursue greatness remained. I excelled throughout and decided to pursue my doctoral degree. The challenges I faced and times I wanted to quit were innumerable. However, in those times, I was reminded of my old mantra "Failure is not an option" and the power of God almighty. Guess what? I made it! So, can you! You are destined for greatness and you are an overcomer.

There will be many times when you feel overwhelmed and unsure but during those times, it is important to rely on the power of God and the power of prayer. I have personally witnessed God move insurmountable obstacles from my path. This book was written to serve as a guide for your journey. My prayer is for you to utilize the strategies, prayers and promises from God to help you evolve as a student nurse and beyond!

~ DAY ONE ~

THE LAW

"Thy word have I hid in mine heart, that I might not sin against thee." KJV-Psalm 119:11

Recently, I went to a new nail salon for a manicure. I noticed immediately how the technician took the time to explain certain things and the need to have the area sanitized. Inquisitive as always, I wondered why I never observed this level of sanitation in other salons. She later explained how many times training in nail care is conducted by family members who show new technicians the procedure. She further explained how they know the law but not the "why" behind the law and for that reason, they become noncompliant. The Spirit of the Lord reminded me in that moment of how, when it comes to the laws of God, we know the law or the word, but we lack awareness of the reason or "why" behind the law. The children of Israel, God's chosen people, struggled with following His word and obeying the law. In fact, the laws of God given to Moses were broken through idol worship before the Lord ever gave them to His people. In the world of nursing, we have expectations for several principles and practices. As you learn your course content always, take a deeper look to learn the why behind the practice. For example, in a simple procedure such as handwashing, "Why don't we touch the faucet again after we have washed our hands? Why do we use a paper towel?" Of course, it is to prevent cross contaminating your hands. When you can answer the "why" behind your content, you will always remember.

Prayer: Father God, in the name of Jesus, Your law is always good and perfect. As I study throughout my nursing journey, help me to hide Your word and "why" in my heart. I believe that with You, all things are possible and I praise You in advance. Amen.

~ DAY TWO ~

THE PROMISE

"In the beginning was the Word, and the Word was with God and, the Word was God." KJV-John 1:1

Over 2,000 years ago on a rugged cross at Calvary, with blood oozing from every orifice of his body, Jesus declared "It is finished!" Those three words finalized every promise, every blessing and every miracle concerning us. There will be times of testing and great stress, especially on your journey to becoming a nurse. During the time of testing, rely on the strength of God and remember His promises. God is faithful and He is with you! He has never made not even one promise that he failed to keep.

Prayer: Father, when my faith is wavering, and my burdens become too much to bear, help me to stand on Your promises. Give me strength in the face of adversity and faith to stand on Your promises. Amen.

~ DAY 3 ~

GOD'S SECRET WEAPON

"But He knoweth the way that I take: when He hath tried me, I shall come forth as gold." KJV-Job 23:10

He was a shepherd boy and small in stature at that. Who was he to take on a giant, a Philistine warrior like Goliath? He faced opposition all around, even his brothers scorned him. But he had a secret. He was God's secret weapon. God was privately preparing him for his purpose. He conquered lions and bears while tending to the sheep. He knew the giant; Goliath was no match for his powerful God. He brought five (the number of grace) smooth stones but he only had to use one. The power was not in the slingshot nor the stone, the power was in the God behind it! His fight was fixed. He has already fixed our fights, and every giant, every adversity, and fear is already defeated. Take comfort in knowing that the Lord is with you.

Prayer: Father, when I am faced with giants and adversity on every hand, help me to remember you won the battle on Calvary. I thank you in advance for total and complete victory. In the name of Jesus, Amen.

~ DAY 4 ~

HE IS GREATER

"And God said unto Moses, I AM THAT I AM: and He said, Thus shalt thou say unto the children of Israel, I AM hath sent me unto you." KJV-Exodus 3:14

He was god or so he thought. He had horses, the fastest chariots and even the mention of his name caused great fear in distant nations. However, there was one greater and his name is, I am that I am. God waged war on Pharaoh and the Egyptian gods. The attacks from God were tailor-made and designed as an attack on each of the different Egyptian gods. The only true and living God, the all-powerful God defeated pharaoh and all the other gods. El Elyon(God most high) was victorious! God was exalted in earth and the heavens. God is exalted above every situation and circumstance. God is the most high. God is faithful to perform His word and He has never lost one fight. In times of testing, always remember He is with you; He is there to strengthen and protect you.

Prayer: Father, you are greater, greater than all my battles. Today, I surrender every worry, every fear and all my circumstances to You. I praise You in advance, in the mighty name of Jesus, Amen.

~ DAY 5 ~

THE WORD

"In the beginning was the Word, and the Word was with God, and the Word was God." KJV-John: 1:1

In the beginning was the Word, and the Word was God. His Word created the sun, moon, stars, creeping things and everything in between. Heaven and Earth may pass away but the Word of the Lord will forever stand. Praying His Word and His promises(scripture), secures victory every single time. He is forever faithful, and His Word is true. Every miracle, every promise, every blessing, and every healing is already done.

Prayer: Father God, your Word is true, and I trust all Your promises concerning me. I will stand on Your Word even in times of testing. Thank you for the power in Your Word, in the name of Jesus, Amen.

~ DAY 6 ~

HE WALKS ON WATER

"And in the fourth watch of the night, Jesus went unto them, walking on the sea. " KJV-Matthew 14:25

He went away privately to pray and sent His disciples away on the boat to cross over to the other side. The winds were high, and the boat was being tossed. Jesus came to them walking on water and Peter asked for permission to come to Him. Peter was able to walk on top of the water as long as he kept his eyes focused on Jesus. As the winds became stronger, he became afraid and started to sink but Jesus caught him as he began to sink. The eyes of the Lord run to and forth throughout the entire Earth to show Himself strong on behalf of those whose heart is perfect (faith and obedience) to him (2 Chronicles 16:9). In all times and in all circumstances, keep your eyes on Jesus as He will not let you sink.

Prayer: Father God, when the winds of life begin to blow, help me to remember You are bigger than any storm. May my faith continually increase each day. Lord, show yourself strong on my behalf and help me to keep my focus on You, in the mighty name of Jesus, Amen.

~ DAY 7 ~

RECOVERING ALL

"And David inquired at the Lord, saying, Shall I pursue after this troop? Shall I overtake them? And He answered him, pursue for thou shalt surely overtake them and without fail recover all." KJV-I Samuel 30:8

King David was perhaps the mightiest king throughout the history of the children of Israel. However, prior to becoming king, there was a time when David lost all his worldly possessions. King David returned to Ziklag and found the city burned and everything he owned taken by his enemies - the Amalekites. The men who were with David spoke of stoning him as they experienced great losses as well. However, David trusted in the Lord. David sent for the priest and the ephod to determine if he should pursue. The Lord told him, "Go for surely you will recover all." David and his men pursued, and he recovered ALL: nothing small or great was missing.

Prayer: Father God, when faced with adversity on every hand, help me to recover all. Lord, I know You are with me, and I will recover all my joy, peace and promises, in the mighty name of Jesus, Amen.

~ DAY 8 ~

DON'T BE AFRAID

"And Moses said unto the people, Fear ye not, stand still and see the salvation of the Lord, which He will shew you today: For the Egyptians whom ye have seen today ye shall see them again no more forever." KJV-Exodus 14:13

It was a beautiful day. They were leaving Egypt and excitement and anticipation was in the air. However, God hardened the heart of Pharaoh and he pursued after them. The children of Israel saw Pharaoh and his chariots and became very afraid. Moses said to the people, "Be not afraid! Stand still and see the salvation of the Lord, which He will accomplish for you today. For the Egyptians you see today you shall see again no more forever. Please do not be afraid when challenges arise. God does not call you to a battle He hasn't equipped you to win. Your victory is secure, stand still and see the salvation of the Lord!

Prayer: Father God, help me today to place all my hope and trust in You. Lord help me to trust Your powerful hand and to know that the enemies of fear, doubt and negativity that I have seen in the past, I will see not again. In the mighty name of Jesus, Amen.

~ DAY 9 ~

SEND UP PRAISE

"Now after the death of Joshua it came to pass, that the children of Israel asked the Lord, saying. Who shall go up for us against the Canaanites first to fight against them? And the Lord said, Judah shall go up: behold, I have delivered the land into his hand." KJV-Judges 1:1-2

They were heading into battle. A battle with the Canaanites who were great in the land. The children of Israel inquired of the Lord who should go up first into the battle against the Canaanites. The Lord answered by saying that the tribe of Judah shall go up: as He had delivered the land into the hands of Judah. Judah means praise! Judah represents prayer, worship and a breakthrough anointing. Jesus, our Savior, the beautiful lion of the tribe of Judah goes before you in every situation. Starting each day with praise prompts our Lord to enter our circumstances with His power.

Prayer: Heavenly Father, help me each day to send forth Judah first through prayer, praise and worship. Father, I ask You to stand with me each day and give me strength. In the mighty name of Jesus, Amen.

~ DAY 10 ~

VICTORY ON THE CROSS

"Jesus, when He had cried again with a loud voice, yielded up the ghost." KJV-Matthew 27:50

On the cross, with the nails placed in His hands and feet, and the crown of thorns on His head, He bled from every orifice of His body. The blood poured down from the cross and onto the ground. A description is provided in Genesis 2:7 which reveals how man was formed from the dust of the ground. After the fall of man in the garden, sin and curses were the consequences. As the ground was cursed, so was humanity. When the blood of Jesus poured onto the ground, it covered every curse that had been placed on man and everything formed from the dust of the ground. The blood covered every manner of sickness, disease, poverty, sin and death. This covering given by Hs blood provides us access to guaranteed victory. The shock of the blood loss and trauma should have killed Him. However, Jesus did not die until He said, "It is finished." Those three words secured our victory forever. Jesus gave up His spirit, the Holy Spirit as His final act to secure our victory. Jesus then rose with all power both in heaven and Earth. He is with us always and through Him because of the cross, we have the victory.

Prayer: Father God, I thank you for Jesus. Thank you, Jesus, for Your precious blood. Help me to remember each day the power of Your blood. Thank you for cleansing me and winning all my victories. In the mighty name of Jesus, Amen.

~ DAY 11 ~

GOD IS WITH YOU

"But my servant Caleb, because he had another spirit with him and hath followed me fully, him will I bring into the land where in he went; and his seed shall possess it." KJV-Numbers 14:24

God almighty led them out of Egypt. He led them out by His presence. Moses sent out 12 spies to view the land. Ten of the spies came back with evil reports, while two of the other spies, Joshua and Caleb, were reported as having another spirit. These two were filled with the Holy Spirit and placed their confidence in God. They believed in their ability through God to conquer the land. The words of the others caused them to see themselves as grasshoppers while being compared to the "giants" in the land. Though circumstances can at times present as giants, there is one who is greater than any circumstance with you. Hold fast in confidence to God and possess your promises because you are well able to overcome.

Prayer: Father God, help me to be encouraged in Your presence. Help me to stand on Your promises in front of the giants I face. I believe that You are all powerful and all my trust is in You. In the mighty name of Jesus, Amen.

~ DAY 12 ~

GOD WHO ANSWERS BY FIRE

God also bearing them witness, both with signs and wonders, and with divers' miracles, and gifts of the Holy Ghost, according to His own will? KJV-Hebrews 2:4

There was a showdown on Mount Carmel. The showdown included 450 prophets of Baal, 400 prophets of Asherah and one prophet of God, Elijah. The God who answered by fire would be God. The prophets of Baal called on their God all day. These prophets stood up on their altar, cut themselves and prophesied until they had no voice. There was no answer. Elijah, the prophet of God, prayed after he filled the wood, trenches and stones with 12 barrels of water. God answered by fire. The fire from God consumed the sacrifice. God's demonstration of fire includes miracles, signs and wonders. He is El Shaddai, Almighty, Sufficient One. God is mighty enough to overcome every battle and enough to be everything you need, and He is with you.

Prayer: Father, You are the God who answers by fire. Help me in times of trouble to rely on Your strength. Thank you for being with me and providing me strength. I will forever praise Your name. In the name of Jesus, Amen.

~ DAY 13 ~

A HEAVENLY HOST IS WITH YOU

"Therefore, David enquired again of God; and God said unto him, go not up after them; turn away from them, and come upon them over against the mulberry trees. And it shall be, when thou shalt hear a sound of going in the tops of the mulberry trees, that then thou shalt go out to battle: for God is gone forth before thee to smite the host of the Philistines." KJV-I Chronicles 14: 14-15

They were headed into battle with the Philistines and David inquired of the Lord if he should attack. The Lord told him, "When you hear the sound of marching atop the mulberry trees then attack, for you will know the Lord goes before you." A heavenly host is with you and they are accompanying you each day. The heavenly host ensures victory as God is with you.

Prayer: Father, I trust Your plans and thank you for sending a heavenly host with me. I commit to You all my dreams and my plans. Thank you for all Your many blessings, and I stand on Your word. In the mighty name of Jesus, Amen.

~ DAY 14 ~

HOPE IN JESUS

May the God of hope fill you with all joy and peace as you trust in him, so that you may overflow with hope by the power of the Holy Spirit NIV- Romans 15:13

Jesus is our hope. In Him we can have both joy and peace in knowing that He never disappoints. There are times when our plans do not work as we expect, yet the plans of God always prevail. Our belief in Jesus also allows us to have confidence in His promises. Jesus allowed us to know that with God all things truly are possible. When hard times arise, and sickness comes, we place all our hope in Jesus, the Savior of the world.

Prayer: Father, in the name of Jesus, all my hope is in You. Help me to trust in Your plans even when the plan differs from my desires. I thank you in advance, in the mighty name of Jesus, Amen.

~ DAY 15 ~

WORDS HAVE POWER

"Death and life are in the power of the tongue: and they that love it shall eat the fruit thereof.:" KJV-Proverbs 18:21

Imagine having an angel dispatched who had the power to make every word you speak happen instantaneously. Sure, we would speak words to declare health, wealth, new homes and cars, and then what? Are you as careful when speaking words when discouraged or feeling hopeless? Well our words have the power to do just what the hypothetical angel would do. Our words have the power to bring blessings or curses, so do not speak it, unless you wish to see it happen.

Prayer: Father, forgive me for the times when I have spoken in doubt and fear. Father set a guard around my mouth and help me to speak by faith even when my way is unclear. Lord, I thank you in advance, in Jesus' name, Amen.

~ WHERE TO BEGIN? ~

NURSING STUDENT TIPS

You have been accepted into nursing school, now what? At this point, I am sure you are excited, yet afraid of the unknown. My goal is to provide you with insight as to the expectations and strategies for success.

- Generally, with your acceptance letter, you will receive instructions which include orientation date.
- Please be sure to read the entire letter and follow instructions.
- Initial requirements/expectations include requirements for textbooks, immunization, CPR and uniforms.

Next, let's think of a few important questions to answer.

Where can I purchase uniforms and books? Check bulletin boards at the school as graduate students often look to sell these items: they are more cost effective. (However, be sure to doublecheck, before purchasing, that no changes have been made).

Have I planned for work, childcare and family obligations? The demands of nursing school cannot be understated and should not be underestimated. A good plan includes a plan and a backup plan. Study time should be built in daily as well as time to prepare for clinical.

What is my plan for organization? Organization is your friend. It is important to create a plan for organizing your study materials and to keep track of important dates. Also, meal planning, and incorporating simple crock pot recipes is another means to organize and provide additional time for study during the week.

~ READY TO LEARN ~

LEARNING STRATEGIES

One of the most important tasks to learn and apply as a nursing student is ***the nursing process***. The nursing process provides the foundation to answer test questions and provide care in the patient setting. What does the nursing process begin with? Assessment!

- ✓ Learning strategy 1 is to conduct a learning style inventory or assessment. This is important as it will provide guidance as to which methods are most effective for you as the learning. **For example:** if you are a kinesthetic learner (learn by doing), it would not be beneficial for you to spend hours reading. It is highly unlikely for you to benefit from this strategy. However, if you were to take the course material into bite-size chunks and apply it by standing or moving when learning new material, then you would likely retain the material. Demonstration and taking frequent breaks to move during study sessions are also helpful for kinesthetic learners.

- ✓ Learning Strategy 2 is to read and prepare before class. Preparing for class allows you the ability to focus on the course instructor and highlight complicated or unfamiliar information. Reading before class provides you with an excellent foundation for learning new course materials.

- ✓ Learning strategy 3 is to create your own strategy for remembering important concepts. One helpful strategy is to use associations. **For example:** I learned as a student to differentiate cholesterol levels by associating them with old cowboy movies. "The bad guys lay low... LDL (low density lipoproteins) are the bad cholesterol." Further, you can make up acronyms or rhymes to facilitate retention of course concepts.

- ✓ Learning strategy 4 is to find a distraction-free environment to learn materials. It is important to determine, early on, if you study best alone or in the presence of a study group. There is not a right or wrong way; do whichever works best for you. **Caution:** When studying in a group, be sure to formulate group goals and focus on the task without distraction.

Here are a few important questions to answer:

How will I prepare for course lectures? Preparing for lecture includes previewing course materials and being prepared to take notes.

How can I ensure I get the most out of lectures?

Preparation is key. By preparing in advance for the lecture, you can focus on the material being presented and clarify confusing or difficult concepts with course faculty.

How can I use my learning style to prepare for lecture and clinical?
Having an awareness of your learning style is of great benefit as it provides the means to help you understand how to make associations or bridge the gap between the classroom and clinical environment.

Are you a good note taker? Note taking is an acquired skill. Due to our society with increased technology, the need to learn note taking has diminished. However, I encourage you to learn how to take notes and identify important concepts.

Dr. Tomekia Tip: When reading your textbook, always remember that tables or charts, items which read "nursing alert" or "key concept" are an excellent source for test questions. Always be sure to read these important items.

~ CLASSROOM 101 ~

CLASSROOM STRATEGIES

Let's think of the classroom as your home away from home. Much of your learning will occur in the classroom. However, it is an expectation of course faculty for you to retain the information provided in the classroom to then translate it all into the clinical environment.

- ✓ Classroom strategy 1 - Attendance is essential. A great part of your success will begin simply with attending class. In the event of a course absence, be sure to let your instructor know and arrange to obtain notes from someone in the course who takes good notes.

- ✓ Classroom strategy 2 - A key strategy to classroom success is to come to class prepared. Previewing notes and course textbook materials cannot be understated. Review the course syllabus, especially the course objectives. Course content and exam questions tie back to course objectives as provided in the syllabus.

- ✓ Classroom strategy 3 - Seating is key. Some schools provide assigned seats while other schools allow individual students to decide. Strategies for seating include sitting near the front - this is a means to avoid distractions, to clearly hear the instructor and imagine the instructor as speaking only to you.

- ✓ Classroom strategy 4 - Notes are important. Identify a method or an outline format to take notes. Always come prepared with enough clean paper and pen/pencils. Write legibly or use an electronic device if allowed. Highlight key concepts* *(more details in the test taking strategies). Learn how to shorthand notes by highlighting or paying attention to focus areas as provided by the course instructor. Ask questions! I can recall as a student being afraid to ask a "dumb question" and instead being silent when I did not understand or needed further clarification on a course concept. However, in hindsight this was not a wise approach. In class, you have an expert faculty available who can guide you through the materials. Take the time to make the most out of every learning opportunity and ask questions.

- ✓ <u>Classroom strategy 5</u> - After class, take a moment to read and organize your class notes. Take the notes and reflect on important concepts then highlight key points. Read and review notes each day to prepare for your exam because it is not advised to cram concepts the night before an exam.

Dr. Tomekia Tip: Pay attention to instructor repetition. Important concepts are often repeated, so ensure that your brain pays attention, circle, underline or highlight concepts.

~ TEST TAKING STRATEGIES ~

TEST TAKING STRATEGIES

As an educator, I have been asked on numerous occasions by students: "Just tell me what's on the test." This seems rather simple on the surface. However, think of each test as being taken directly at the bedside. You are basically asking the instructor, when you are standing at the bedside with a patient depending on you: "Just tell me what to do to save their life." This provides a different outlook doesn't it?

In my experience, most students do not struggle with content. Have you studied hours upon hours, and memorized chapter content? Yet, when test scores are reviewed, it does not reflect your knowledge of the content. That's because the struggle is not with the content: it is with being able to apply the concepts. Let's discuss a few strategies...

- ✓ <u>Test taking strategy 1-</u> Remember the nursing process. Generally, nursing questions are written, and the options are developed using the nursing process. Answers on nursing exams and the NCLEX® are written within the scope of nursing practice. Through process of elimination based upon information presented, it is determined which action is suitable. **Example:** read the answer stem, be sure you have a clear understanding of what the question is asking. Then, if enough information is provided in the stem to provide a clear picture of the patient, then we know an assessment answer is unlikely. Our answer choice would likely be an intervention or nursing action.

- ✓ <u>Test taking strategy 2 -</u> Only consider information as provided in the question stem. Do not make assumptions or read into questions. Along with this, go with your first mind. In reading a question if an answer immediately jumps out at you, then likely you are recalling something previously read or learned. The trick is remembering not to change your answer or talk yourself out of your first mind.

- ✓ <u>Test taking strategy 3 -</u> Patient safety is always a priority. The care of the patient is decided after the condition of the patient is identified. Remember the ABCs….

- ✓ <u>Test taking strategy 4 -</u> In some instances, multiple or all answer choices are correct. In this instance, which answer choice is priority? Priority is determined based on patients' conditions and outcomes (SAFETY).

- ✓ <u>Test taking strategy 5 -</u> Practice, practice, practice. Practice questions are very helpful. Textbooks generally come with online resources to include test banks and other invaluable resources. A key strategy is to review practice questions and understand rationales as this further helps to facilitate the learning process.

Dr. Tomekia Tip: The best test preparation includes studying in advance. Begin with syllabus and work through the course objectives. Preparation is a marathon, not a sprint, therefore, cramming and procrastination are recipes for disaster; they create anxiety and pressure. Also, when considering test items, always reflect on the rationale. Having an awareness of the rationale allows you to understand the "why" behind the concept.

~ CLINICAL STRATEGIES ~

CLINICAL STRATEGIES

Clinical for some students is a great source of anxiety, while other students absolutely love the clinical environment. In this environment, preparation is again key. Critical thinking and utilizing the nursing process are helpful in preparing for the clinical day.

- ✓ Clinical strategy 1 - Clinical paperwork is key. Remember that the paperwork provides a picture and the picture should be detailed enough for the instructor to visualize the patient without ever entering the room. How is this possible? The steps of the nursing process should be used, especially in an assessment in order to "paint the canvas."

- ✓ Clinical strategy 2 - Dress to impress. Remember, appearances often speak louder than words. In preparation, be sure to have the clinical attire well kempt by being clean and neatly pressed.

- ✓ Clinical strategy 3 - Review skills in the days leading up to clinical. Do not shy away from learning experiences as this is the opportunity to learn or brush up on skills. In preparation, review skills that are challenging to you and seek out new opportunities to learn how to perform the skill. Be sure to communicate with your instructor in relation to a need to experience a skill.

- ✓ Clinical strategy 4 - Always remember the rights of patient medication administration because safety is a priority. In preparing for the clinical day, review patient medications and pay attention to pharmacology, in particular, lab values, allergies and special precautions.

~ SPECIAL TIPS FOR ADVANCED PRACTICE NURSING STUDENTS~

TIPS FOR ADVANCING IN NURSING

We are now amid an exciting time to be a nurse. In our present time, nurses are now entrepreneurs, coaches, speakers and educators. Nursing is on track to advance with new doors of opportunity opening quickly and nurses are now returning to school and, seeking advanced education in increasing numbers. I am amongst that population, as my career began as an associate degree nurse. Here are my top tips for nurses who wish to advance.

- ✓ Advanced nursing tip 1 - Seek the Lord and be sure it is a God-given idea. I have learned through life and experience that every good idea is not a God ordained idea. Allow the Lord to guide you in whatever direction that leads to your purpose. During this time, here are a few helpful questions to ponder.

    What are my long-term goals? How does pursuing advanced education tie into this goal?

    What is my motivation to pursue this goal?

    Will this goal lead or facilitate my God-given purpose?

    Have I set aside time for studying and clinical activities?

    Have I considered the possibility of decreased work scheduling or the need to change career paths, while pursuing the goal?

- ✓ Advanced nursing tip 2 - Identify your top three choices for schools and research admission criteria. In the event of needing a GRE score, utilize a practice book. Also, it is helpful to read scholarly journals and articles to become familiar with lingo. Along with this, practice timed writing exercises as these are very helpful to condition you for the writing requirements of the GRE and advanced nursing education.

- ✓ <u>Advanced nursing tip 3</u> – Identify your area of interest early in the learning process and build a stockpile of scholarly articles and resources. This will help with the scholarly project or dissertation project.

- ✓ <u>Advanced nursing tip 4</u> – Networking is extremely helpful. Throughout the course of study, you will likely need nurses to serve as preceptors and mentors. Take time to intentionally network as this will help you in building a community of potential mentors and preceptors.

- ✓ <u>Advanced nursing tip 5</u> - Apply for every scholarship available. Seriously, apply. Often, many scholarships are unawarded or awarded by default due to the slim applicant pool.

- ✓ <u>Advanced nursing tip 6</u> - When selecting your topic of interest for your thesis, capstone, dissertation or scholarly project, select a topic in which you are extremely interested. In selecting a topic, you are passionate about, this will provide you the stamina needed to complete the project. Also, you will be known in scholarly communities as an expert on the subject matter.

~ PRAYER & AFFIRMATIONS ~

FUTURE NURSE'S PRAYER

Heavenly Father, thank You for all Your many blessings. Thank You for Your Son who shed His blood just for me. Thank You for every blessing, both great and small. Lord, thank You for this divine calling to serve others and to be your hands and feet on this Earth. As I journey through school, allow your precious Holy Spirit to guide me. Help me to excel academically and clinically. Lord, bring all things back to my remembrance. Help me to remember daily, my ability to touch lives. Guide my hands, and my heart throughout this journey. I am who you say I am! And whatever things you ask in prayer, believing, you will receive. Matthew 21:22

Believe it and Receive it! I can have what you say I can have! I will be what You say I will be! In the precious name of Jesus,

AMEN

PRAYER FOR NURSES

Father God, in the name of Jesus, You are the source of my strength and I thank You for my divine calling to serve others. Prepare me so I can serve each day with the humility of Christ. Help me to comfort all who are in need and give me wisdom with my words. When I am unsure of my direction, help me to seek Your wisdom, and find comfort in You. Open my heart to the needs of others and help me to provide compassionate care when it is needed most. Let me display Your love and serve as Your hands and feet here on Earth, in the mighty name of Jesus, **Amen.**

AFFIRMATIONS FOR NURSES

- **I am blessed and highly favored!** The favor and blessings of God are upon me.

- **I am focused and ready to slay today!** Today, my mind is focused and I can handle whatever this day brings through Christ (Philippians 4:13).

- **I am striving each day to be the best nurse I can be!** I am created to serve and I will provide excellent nursing care.

- **I am filled with the joy and peace of the Lord!** God is my peace and He brings the fullness of joy into my life.

- **I am healthy and my mind is brilliant!** God strengthens my body and mind each day.

SALVATION PRAYER

Father God, I have tried it my way and failed. I know that I am a sinner in need of salvation. No longer will I do it my way, so I ask You to take the lead and guide me throughout my life. In faith, I accept the gift of salvation made possible through the precious blood of Jesus on the cross. I now accept You as Lord and Savior of my life. Thank you Father for sending Jesus. I believe that You, Jesus, are the son of God who died on the cross for my sins and rose from the dead on the third day. Thank You for bearing my sins, and the cross that I could not bear. Thank You for the gift of eternal life. I believe Your words are true and I accept You as the power source in my life. Come into my heart, Lord Jesus and be my savior.

Amen

PRAYER FOR ENCOURAGEMENT

Heavenly Father, thank You for taking the lead in my life. Thank You for being here when I am lost, discouraged and afraid. Help me to be renewed in heart and mind, each and every day. Encourage my heart through Your word. Lord, grant me strength to make it through this day. I will forever sing Your praises, in Jesus' mighty name,

Amen

7 KEYS TO BUILDING YOUR RELATIONSHIP WITH THE HOLY SPIRIT

- ✓ **Become aware:** Make yourself aware. He lives on the inside of you and He longs to commune with you daily. **"And I will ask the Father, and He will give you another advocate to help you and be with you forever— the Spirit of truth. The world cannot accept Him because it neither sees Him nor knows Him.** *But you know Him, for He lives with You and will be in You.* **(John 14:16-17)**

- ✓ **Believe:** Believing is very important. Unbelief hinders the very possibility of your prayers and relationship with Him. And without faith, it is impossible to please God because *anyone who comes to Him, must believe that He exists and that He rewards those who earnestly seek Him*. **(Hebrews 11:6).**

- ✓ **Worship:** Worship is the key that unlocks the door into His presence. Take time to worship Him not for what He has or can do for you but simply because of who He is. Enter His gates with thanksgiving and His courts with praise; *give thanks to Him and praise His name.* **(Psalm 100:4)**

- ✓ **Prayer:** Prayer is an important component of daily fellowship. Pray and speak His promises and will for your life. His promises and will are found in the word of God. This is the confidence we have in approaching God: that *if we ask anything according to his will, He hears us.*(**1 John 5:14)**

- ✓ **Spend time with Him:** Take the initiative to carve out time daily to get to know him. Learn His voice and pursue Him **(He is a person, not an IT or THING!!)** When the Advocate comes, whom I will send to you from the Father—the Spirit of truth who goes out from the Father—***He will testify about me.*** **(John 15:26)**

- ✓ **Have no other God before Him**: He is the only one who can fill all of your voids. He is the answer to everything you have ever desired or longed for. The fullness of joy is found with Him. Jesus replied: "'***Love the Lord your God with all your heart and with all your soul and with all your mind.*** **(Matthew 22:37)**

- ✓ **Avoid behaviors that grieve Him:** Grieving Him extends beyond the obvious sins of the flesh that we ordinarily think on. Grieving Him can occur when we do not love right, when we walk in unforgiveness, when we gossip and when we choose to live our lives in an unholy manner. We must make the choice daily to embrace His love, seek forgiveness and be cleansed continuously in the precious blood of Jesus. And ***do not grieve the Holy Spirit of God***, with whom you were sealed for the day of redemption. **(Ephesians 4:30)**

SCRIPTURES TO RENEW HOPE

- ✓ But those **who hope in the Lord will renew their strength**. They will soar on wings like eagles; they will run and not grow weary, they will walk and not be faint. **(Isaiah 40:31)**

- ✓ And the God of all grace, who called you to His eternal glory in Christ, after you have suffered a little while, will **Himself restore you and make you strong, firm and steadfast**. **(I Peter 5:10)**

- ✓ And **hope does not put us to shame** because God's love has been poured out into our hearts through the Holy Spirit, who has been given to us. **(Romans 5:5)**

- ✓ May the **God of hope** fill you with all joy and peace as you trust in Him, so that you may **overflow with hope by the power of the Holy Spirit.** **(Romans 15:13)**

- ✓ Oh, that **I might have my request**, God would grant **what I hope for**. **(Job 6:8)**

- ✓ Be strong and take heart, all you **who hope in the Lord.** **(Psalm 31:24)**

- ✓ Trust **in the Lord with all your heart** and lean not on your own understanding. In all your ways submit to Him and **He will make your paths straight**. **(Proverbs 3:5-6)**

- ✓ **Peace I leave with you; my peace I give you**. I do not give to you as the world gives. **Do not let your hearts be troubled and do not be afraid**. **(John 14:27)**

- ✓ For the Spirit God gave us does not make us timid **but gives us power, love and self-discipline.** **(2 Timothy 1:7)**

Made in the USA
Columbia, SC
28 March 2022